The Waste Land

By T. S. Eliot

T. S. ELIOT

The Waste Land

with an afterword to
the 75th anniversary edition by
CHRISTOPHER RICKS

A HARVEST BOOK
HARCOURT BRACE & COMPANY
San Diego   New York   London

ISBN 0-15-600534-4

Text set in Fournier
Designed by Kaelin Chappell
Printed in the United States of America

A C E F D B

The Waste Land

The Waste Land

1922

'Nam Sibyllam quidem Cumis ego ipse oculis meis
vidi in ampulla pendere, et cum illi pueri dicerent:
Σίβυλλα τί θέλεις; respondebat illa:ἀποθανεῖν θέλω.'

For Ezra Pound
il miglior fabbro

April is the cruellest month, breeding
Lilacs out of the dead land, mixing
Memory and desire, stirring
Dull roots with spring rain.
Winter kept us warm, covering
Earth in forgetful snow, feeding
A little life with dried tubers.
Summer surprised us, coming over the
     Starnbergersee
With a shower of rain; we stopped in the colonnade,
And went on in sunlight, into the Hofgarten,   10
And drank coffee, and talked for an hour.
Bin gar keine Russin, stamm' aus Litauen, echt
     deutsch.
And when we were children, staying at the arch-
     duke's,
My cousin's, he took me out on a sled,
And I was frightened. He said, Marie,

3

Marie, hold on tight. And down we went.
In the mountains, there you feel free.
I read, much of the night, and go south in the winter.

What are the roots that clutch, what branches
    grow
Out of this stony rubbish? Son of man,   20
You cannot say, or guess, for you know only
A heap of broken images, where the sun beats,
And the dead tree gives no shelter, the cricket no relief,
And the dry stone no sound of water. Only
There is shadow under this red rock,
(Come in under the shadow of this red rock),
And I will show you something different from either
Your shadow at morning striding behind you
Or your shadow at evening rising to meet you;
I will show you fear in a handful of dust.   30

> *Frisch weht der Wind*
> *Der Heimat zu*
> *Mein Irisch Kind,*
> *Wo weilest du?*

'You give me hyacinths first a year ago;
'They call me the hyacinth girl.'

4

—Yet when we came back, late, from the hyacinth
    garden,
Your arms full, and your hair wet, I could not
Speak, and my eyes failed, I was neither
Living nor dead, and I knew nothing,   40
Looking into the heart of light, the silence.
Oed' und leer das Meer.

    Madame Sosostris, famous clairvoyante,
Had a bad cold, nevertheless
Is known to be the wisest woman in Europe,
With a wicked pack of cards. Here, said she,
Is your card, the drowned Phoenician Sailor,
(Those are pearls that were his eyes. Look!)
Here is Belladonna, the Lady of the Rocks,
The lady of situations.   50
Here is the man with three staves, and here the
    Wheel,
And here is the one-eyed merchant, and this card,
Which is blank, is something he carries on his back,
Which I am forbidden to see. I do not find
The Hanged Man. Fear death by water.
I see crowds of people, walking round in a ring.

Thank you. If you see dear Mrs. Equitone,
Tell her I bring the horoscope myself:
One must be so careful these days.

    Unreal City, 60
Under the brown fog of a winter dawn,
A crowd flowed over London Bridge, so many,
I had not thought death had undone so many.
Sighs, short and infrequent, were exhaled,
And each man fixed his eyes before his feet.
Flowed up the hill and down King William Street,
To where Saint Mary Woolnoth kept the hours
With a dead sound on the final stroke of nine.
There I saw one I knew, and stopped him, crying: 'Stetson!
'You who were with me in the ships at Mylae! 70
'That corpse you planted last year in your garden,
'Has it begun to sprout? Will it bloom this year?
'Or has the sudden frost disturbed its bed?
'O keep the Dog far hence, that's friend to men,
'Or with his nails he'll dig it up again!
'You! hypocrite lecteur!—mon semblable,—mon frère!'

The Chair she sat in, like a burnished throne,
Glowed on the marble, where the glass
Held up by standards wrought with fruited vines
From which a golden Cupidon peeped out   80
(Another hid his eyes behind his wing)
Doubled the flames of sevenbranched candelabra
Reflecting light upon the table as
The glitter of her jewels rose to meet it,
From satin cases poured in rich profusion.
In vials of ivory and coloured glass
Unstoppered, lurked her strange synthetic perfumes,
Unguent, powdered, or liquid—troubled, confused
And drowned the sense in odours; stirred by the air
That freshened from the window, these ascended   90
In fattening the prolonged candle-flames,
Flung their smoke into the laquearia,
Stirring the pattern on the coffered ceiling.
Huge sea-wood fed with copper
Burned green and orange, framed by the coloured
        stone,
In which sad light a carvèd dolphin swam.

Above the antique mantel was displayed
As though a window gave upon the sylvan scene
The change of Philomel, by the barbarous king
So rudely forced; yet there the nightingale   100
Filled all the desert with inviolable voice
And still she cried, and still the world pursues,
'Jug Jug' to dirty ears.
And other withered stumps of time
Were told upon the walls; staring forms
Leaned out, leaning, hushing the room enclosed.
Footsteps shuffled on the stair.
Under the firelight, under the brush, her hair
Spread out in fiery points
Glowed into words, then would be savagely still.   110

   'My nerves are bad to-night. Yes, bad. Stay with
        me.
'Speak to me. Why do you never speak. Speak.
   'What are you thinking of? What thinking? What?
'I never know what you are thinking. Think.'

I think we are in rats' alley
Where the dead men lost their bones.

'What is that noise?'
                    The wind under the door.
'What is that noise now? What is the wind doing?'
                    Nothing again nothing.   120
                              'Do
'You know nothing? Do you see nothing? Do you
      remember
'Nothing?'

    I remember
Those are pearls that were his eyes.
'Are you alive, or not? Is there nothing in your
      head?'

                                                        But
O O O O that Shakespeherian Rag—
It's so elegant
So intelligent   130
'What shall I do now? What shall I do?'
'I shall rush out as I am, and walk the street

'With my hair down, so. What shall we do
    to-morrow?
'What shall we ever do?'

                        The hot water at ten.
And if it rains, a closed car at four.
And we shall play a game of chess,
Pressing lidless eyes and waiting for a knock upon the
    door.

    When Lil's husband got demobbed, I said—
I didn't mince my words, I said to her myself,   140
Hurry up please its time
Now Albert's coming back, make yourself a bit smart.
He'll want to know what you done with that money he
    gave you
To get yourself some teeth. He did, I was there.
You have them all out, Lil, and get a nice set,
He said, I swear, I can't bear to look at you.
And no more can't I, I said, and think of poor Albert,
He's been in the army four years, he wants a good
    time,
And if you don't give it him, there's others will, I said.
Oh is there, she said. Something o' that, I said.   150

Then I'll know who to thank, she said, and give me a
    straight look.

HURRY UP PLEASE ITS TIME

If you don't like it you can get on with it, I said.

Others can pick and choose if you can't.

But if Albert makes off, it won't be for lack of telling.

You ought to be ashamed, I said, to look so antique.

(And her only thirty-one.)

I can't help it, she said, pulling a long face,

It's them pills I took, to bring it off, she said.

(She's had five already, and nearly died of young
    George.)   160

The chemist said it would be all right, but I've never
    been the same.

You *are* a proper fool, I said.

Well, if Albert won't leave you alone, there it is, I said,

What you get married for if you don't want children?

HURRY UP PLEASE ITS TIME

Well, that Sunday Albert was home, they had a hot
    gammon,

And they asked me in to dinner, to get the beauty of it
    hot—

HURRY UP PLEASE ITS TIME

Goonight Bill. Goonight Lou. Goonight May.
Goonight.   170
Ta ta. Goonight. Goonight.
Good night, ladies, good night, sweet ladies, good
night, good night.

III. THE FIRE SERMON

The river's tent is broken; the last fingers of leaf
Clutch and sink into the wet bank. The wind
Crosses the brown land, unheard. The nymphs are
departed.
Sweet Thames, run softly, till I end my song.
The river bears no empty bottles, sandwich papers,
Silk handkerchiefs, cardboard boxes, cigarette ends
Or other testimony of summer nights. The nymphs
are departed.
And their friends, the loitering heirs of City
directors;   180
Departed, have left no addresses.
By the waters of Leman I sat down and wept . . .
Sweet Thames, run softly till I end my song,

Sweet Thames, run softly, for I speak not loud or
    long.
But at my back in a cold blast I hear
The rattle of the bones, and chuckle spread from ear
    to ear.

A rat crept softly through the vegetation
Dragging its slimy belly on the bank
While I was fishing in the dull canal
On a winter evening round behind the gashouse   190
Musing upon the king my brother's wreck
And on the king my father's death before him.
White bodies naked on the low damp ground
And bones cast in a little low dry garret,
Rattled by the rat's foot only, year to year.
But at my back from time to time I hear
The sound of horns and motors, which shall bring
Sweeney to Mrs. Porter in the spring.
O the moon shone bright on Mrs. Porter
And on her daughter   200
They wash their feet in soda water
Et O ces voix d'enfants, chantant dans la coupole!

Twit twit twit

Jug jug jug jug jug jug

So rudely forc'd.

Tereu

    Unreal City

Under the brown fog of a winter noon

Mr. Eugenides, the Smyrna merchant

Unshaven, with a pocket full of currants   210

C.i.f. London: documents at sight,

Asked me in demotic French

To luncheon at the Cannon Street Hotel

Followed by a weekend at the Metropole.

    At the violet hour, when the eyes and back

Turn upward from the desk, when the human engine

      waits

Like a taxi throbbing waiting,

I Tiresias, though blind, throbbing between two lives,

Old man with wrinkled female breasts, can see

At the violet hour, the evening hour that strives   220

Homeward, and brings the sailor home from sea,

The typist home at teatime, clears her breakfast, lights
     Her stove, and lays out food in tins.
Out of the window perilously spread
Her drying combinations touched by the sun's last rays,
     On the divan are piled (at night her bed)
Stockings, slippers, camisoles, and stays.
I Tiresias, old man with wrinkled dugs
Perceived the scene, and foretold the rest—
I too awaited the expected guest.   230
He, the young man carbuncular, arrives,
A small house agent's clerk, with one bold stare,
One of the low on whom assurance sits
As a silk hat on a Bradford millionaire.
The time is now propitious, as he guesses,
The meal is ended, she is bored and tired,
Endeavours to engage her in caresses
Which still are unreproved, if undesired.
Flushed and decided, he assaults at once;
Exploring hands encounter no defence;   240
His vanity requires no response,

And makes a welcome of indifference.
(And I Tiresias have foresuffered all
Enacted on this same divan or bed;
I who have sat by Thebes below the wall
And walked among the lowest of the dead.)
Bestows one final patronising kiss,
And gropes his way, finding the stairs unlit . . .

    She turns and looks a moment in the glass,
Hardly aware of her departed lover;   250
Her brain allows one half-formed thought to pass:
'Well now that's done: and I'm glad it's over.'
When lovely woman stoops to folly and
Paces about her room again, alone,
She smoothes her hair with automatic hand,
And puts a record on the gramophone.

    'This music crept by me upon the waters'
And along the Strand, up Queen Victoria Street.
O City city, I can sometimes hear
Beside a public bar in Lower Thames Street,   260
The pleasant whining of a mandoline
And a clatter and a chatter from within

Where fishmen lounge at noon: where the walls

Of Magnus Martyr hold

Inexplicable splendour of Ionian white and gold.

　　The river sweats

　　Oil and tar

　　The barges drift

　　With the turning tide

　　Red sails　　　　　　　　　　　　270

　　Wide

　　To leeward, swing on the heavy spar.

　　The barges wash

　　Drifting logs

　　Down Greenwich reach

　　Past the Isle of Dogs.

　　　　　　　Weialala leia

　　　　　　　Wallala leialala

　　Elizabeth and Leicester

　　Beating oars　　　　　　　　　　　280

　　The stern was formed

　　A gilded shell

　　Red and gold

The brisk swell
Rippled both shores
Southwest wind
Carried down stream
The peal of bells
White towers

        Weialala leia   290
        Wallala leialala

'Trams and dusty trees.
Highbury bore me. Richmond and Kew
Undid me. By Richmond I raised my knees
Supine on the floor of a narrow canoe.'

'My feet are at Moorgate, and my heart
Under my feet. After the event
He wept. He promised "a new start."
I made no comment. What should I resent?'

'On Margate Sands.   300
I can connect
Nothing with nothing.

The broken fingernails of dirty hands.
My people humble people who expect
Nothing.'

        la la

To Carthage then I came

Burning burning burning burning
O Lord Thou pluckest me out
O Lord Thou pluckest   310

burning

IV. DEATH BY WATER

Phlebas the Phoenician, a fortnight dead,
Forgot the cry of gulls, and the deep sea swell
And the profit and loss.
                      A current under sea
Picked his bones in whispers. As he rose and fell
He passed the stages of his age and youth
Entering the whirlpool.

Gentile or Jew

O you who turn the wheel and look to
    windward,   320
Consider Phlebas, who was once handsome and tall
    as you.

V. WHAT THE THUNDER SAID

    After the torchlight red on sweaty faces
After the frosty silence in the gardens
After the agony in stony places
The shouting and the crying
Prison and palace and reverberation
Of thunder of spring over distant mountains
He who was living is now dead
We who were living are now dying
With a little patience   330

    Here is no water but only rock
Rock and no water and the sandy road
The road winding above among the mountains
Which are mountains of rock without water

If there were water we should stop and drink
Amongst the rock one cannot stop or think
Sweat is dry and feet are in the sand
If there were only water amongst the rock
Dead mountain mouth of carious teeth that cannot
    spit
Here one can neither stand nor lie nor sit   340
There is not even silence in the mountains
But dry sterile thunder without rain
There is not even solitude in the mountains
But red sullen faces sneer and snarl
From doors of mudcracked houses
                            If there were water
   And no rock
   If there were rock
   And also water
   And water   350
   A spring
   A pool among the rock
   If there were the sound of water only
   Not the cicada
   And dry grass singing

But sound of water over a rock
Where the hermit-thrush sings in the pine trees
Drip drop drip drop drop drop drop
But there is no water

Who is the third who walks always beside
   you?   360
When I count, there are only you and I together
But when I look ahead up the white road
There is always another one walking beside you
Gliding wrapt in a brown mantle, hooded
I do not know whether a man or a woman
—But who is that on the other side of you?

What is that sound high in the air
Murmur of maternal lamentation
Who are those hooded hordes swarming
Over endless plains, stumbling in cracked earth   370
Ringed by the flat horizon only
What is the city over the mountains
Cracks and reforms and bursts in the violet air
Falling towers

Jerusalem Athens Alexandria
Vienna London
Unreal

A woman drew her long black hair out tight
And fiddled whisper music on those strings
And bats with baby faces in the violet light   380
Whistled, and beat their wings
And crawled head downward down a blackened wall
And upside down in air were towers
Tolling reminiscent bells, that kept the hours
And voices singing out of empty cisterns and
        exhausted wells.

In this decayed hole among the mountains
In the faint moonlight, the grass is singing
Over the tumbled graves, about the chapel
There is the empty chapel, only the wind's home.
It has no windows, and the door swings,   390
Dry bones can harm no one.
Only a cock stood on the rooftree

Co co rico co co rico

In a flash of lightning. Then a damp gust

Bringing rain

   Ganga was sunken, and the limp leaves

Waited for rain, while the black clouds

Gathered far distant, over Himavant.

The jungle crouched, humped in silence.

Then spoke the thunder   400

DA

Datta: what have we given?

My friend, blood shaking my heart

The awful daring of a moment's surrender

Which an age of prudence can never retract

By this, and this only, we have existed

Which is not to be found in our obituaries

Or in memories draped by the beneficent spider

Or under seals broken by the lean solicitor

In our empty rooms   410

DA

Dayadhvam: I have heard the key

Turn in the door once and turn once only

We think of the key, each in his prison

Thinking of the key, each confirms a prison
Only at nightfall, aethereal rumours
Revive for a moment a broken Coriolanus
DA
Damyata: The boat responded
Gaily, to the hand expert with sail and oar   420
The sea was calm, your heart would have responded
Gaily, when invited, beating obedient
To controlling hands

                                        I sat upon the shore
Fishing, with the arid plain behind me
Shall I at least set my lands in order?
London Bridge is falling down falling down falling
      down
Poi s'ascose nel foco che gli affina
Quando fiam uti chelidon—O swallow swallow
Le Prince d'Aquitaine à la tour abolie   430
These fragments I have shored against my ruins
Why then Ile fit you. Hieronymo's mad againe.
Datta. Dayadhvam. Damyata.
            Shantih   shantih   shantih

NOTES ON
'THE WASTE LAND'

Not only the title, but the plan and a good deal of the incidental symbolism of the poem were suggested by Miss Jessie L. Weston's book on the Grail legend: *From Ritual to Romance* (Cambridge). Indeed, so deeply am I indebted, Miss Weston's book will elucidate the difficulties of the poem much better than my notes can do; and I recommend it (apart from the great interest of the book itself) to any who think such elucidation of the poem worth the trouble. To another work of anthropology I am indebted in general, one which has influenced our generation profoundly; I mean *The Golden Bough*; I have used especially two volumes *Adonis, Attis, Osiris*. Anyone who is acquainted with these works will immediately recognise in the poem certain references to vegetation ceremonies.

Line 20. Cf. Ezekiel II, i.

23. Cf. Ecclesiastes XII, v.

31. V. *Tristan und Isolde*, I, verses 5–8.

42. Id. III, verse 24.

46. I am not familiar with the exact constitution of the Tarot pack of cards, from which I have obviously departed to suit my own convenience. The Hanged Man, a member of the traditional pack, fits my purpose in two ways: because he is associated in my mind with the Hanged God of Frazer, and because I associate him with the hooded figure in the passage of the disciples to Emmaus in Part V. The Phoenician Sailor and the Merchant appear later; also the 'crowds of people,' and Death by Water is executed in Part IV. The Man with Three Staves (an authentic member of the Tarot pack) I associate, quite arbitrarily, with the Fisher King himself.

60. Cf. Baudelaire:

> 'Fourmillante cité, cité pleine de rêves,
> 'Où le spectre en plein jour raccroche le
>   passant.'

63. Cf. *Inferno*, III, 55–57:

>   'si lunga tratta
>
> di gente, ch'io non averei mai creduto
>
> che morte tanta n'avesse disfatta.'

64. Cf. *Inferno*, IV, 25–27:

> 'Quivi, secondo che per ascoltare,
>
> 'non avea pianto, mai che di sospiri
>
> 'che l'aura eterna facevan tremare.'

68. A phenomenon which I have often noticed.

74. Cf. the Dirge in Webster's *White Devil*.

76. V. Baudelaire, Preface to *Fleurs du Mal*.

II. A GAME OF CHESS

77. Cf. *Antony and Cleopatra*, II, ii, l. 190.

92. Laquearia. V. *Aeneid*, I, 726:

> dependent lychni laquearibus aureis incensi, et

noctem flammis funalia vincunt.

98. Sylvan scene. V. Milton, *Paradise Lost*, IV, 140.

99. V. Ovid, *Metamorphoses*, VI, Philomela.

100. Cf. Part III, l. 204.

115. Cf. Part III, l. 195.

118. Cf. Webster: 'Is the wind in that door still?'

126. Cf. Part I, l. 37, 48.

138. Cf. the game of chess in Middleton's *Women beware Women*.

III. THE FIRE SERMON

176. V. Spenser, *Prothalamion*.

192. Cf. *The Tempest*, I, ii.

196. Cf. Marvell, *To His Coy Mistress*.

197. Cf. Day, *Parliament of Bees*:

> 'When of the sudden, listening, you shall hear,
> 'A noise of horns and hunting, which shall
>> bring
> 'Actaeon to Diana in the spring,
> 'Where all shall see her naked skin . . .'

199. I do not know the origin of the ballad from which these lines are taken: it was reported to me from Sydney, Australia.

202. V. Verlaine, *Parsifal*.

210. The currants were quoted at a price 'cost insurance and freight to London'; and the Bill of Lading, etc., were to be handed to the buyer upon payment of the sight draft.

218. Tiresias, although a mere spectator and not

indeed a 'character,' is yet the most important person-
age in the poem, uniting all the rest. Just as the one-
eyed merchant, seller of currants, melts into the
Phoenician Sailor, and the latter is not wholly distinct
from Ferdinand Prince of Naples, so all the women
are one woman, and the two sexes meet in Tiresias.
What Tiresias *sees*, in fact, is the substance of the
poem. The whole passage from Ovid is of great an-
thropological interest:

'. . . Cum Iunone iocos et major vestra profecto est

Quam quae contingit maribus', dixisse, 'voluptas.'

Illa negat; placuit quae sit sententia docti

Quaerere Tiresiae: venus huic erat utraque nota.

Nam duo magnorum viridi coeuntia silva

Corpora serpentum baculi violaverat ictu

Deque viro factus, mirabile, femina septem

Egerat autumnos; octavo rursus eosdem

Vidit et 'est vestrae si tanta potentia plagae',

Dixit 'ut auctoris sortem in contraria mutet,

Nunc quoque vos feriam!' percussis anguibus

     isdem

Forma prior rediit genetivaque venit imago.

Arbiter hic igitur sumptus de lite iocosa

Dicta Iovis firmat; gravius Saturnia iusto

Nec pro materia fertur doluisse suique

Iudicis aeterna damnavit lumina nocte,

At pater omnipotens (neque enim licet inrita cuiquam

    cuiquam

Facta dei fecisse deo) pro lumine adempto

Scire futura dedit poenamque levavit honore.

221. This may not appear as exact as Sappho's lines, but I had in mind the 'longshore' or 'dory' fisherman, who returns at nightfall.

253. V. Goldsmith, the song in *The Vicar of Wakefield*.

257. V. *The Tempest*, as above.

264. The interior of St. Magnus Martyr is to my mind one of the finest among Wren's interiors. See *The Proposed Demolition of Nineteen City Churches*: (P. S. King & Son, Ltd.).

266. The Song of the (three) Thames-daughters begins here. From line 292 to 306 inclusive they speak in turn. V. *Götterdämmerung*, III, i: the Rhine-daughters.

279. V. Froude, *Eliȝabeth*, Vol. I, ch. iv, letter of De Quadra to Philip of Spain:

'In the afternoon we were in a barge, watching the games on the river. (The Queen) was alone with Lord Robert and myself on the poop, when they began to talk nonsense, and went so far that Lord Robert at last said, as I was on the spot there was no reason why they should not be married if the queen pleased.'

293. Cf. *Purgatorio*, V, 133:

> 'Ricorditi di me, che son la Pia;
>
> 'Siena mi fe,' disfecemi Maremma.'

307. V. St. Augustine's *Confessions*: 'to Carthage then I came, where a cauldron of unholy loves sang all about mine ears.'

308. The complete text of the Buddha's Fire Sermon (which corresponds in importance to the Sermon on the Mount) from which these words are taken, will be found translated in the late Henry Clarke Warren's *Buddhism in Translation* (Harvard Oriental Series). Mr. Warren was one of the great pioneers of Buddhist studies in the Occident.

309. From St. Augustine's *Confessions* again. The collocation of these two representatives of eastern and western asceticism, as the culmination of this part of the poem, is not an accident.

In the first part of Part V three themes are employed: the journey to Emmaus, the approach to the Chapel Perilous (see Miss Weston's book) and the present decay of eastern Europe.

357. This is *Turdus aonalaschkae pallasii*, the hermit-thrush which I have heard in Quebec Province. Chapman says (*Handbook of Birds of Eastern North America*) 'it is most at home in secluded woodland and thickety retreats. . . . Its notes are not remarkable for variety or volume, but in purity and sweetness of tone and exquisite modulation they are unequalled.' Its 'water-dripping song' is justly celebrated.

360. The following lines were stimulated by the account of one of the Antarctic expeditions (I forget which, but I think one of Shackleton's): it was related that the party of explorers, at the extremity of their strength, had the constant delusion that there was *one more member* than could actually be counted.

367–77. Cf. Hermann Hesse, *Blick ins Chaos*: 'Schon ist halb Europa, schon ist zumindest der halbe Osten Europas auf dem Wege zum Chaos, fährt betrunken im heiligen Wahn am Abgrund entlang und singt dazu, singt betrunken und hymnisch wie Dmitri Karamasoff sang. Ueber diese Lieder lacht der Bürger beleidigt, der Heilige und Seher hört sie mit Tränen.'

402. 'Datta, dayadhvam, damyata' (Give, sympathise, control). The fable of the meaning of the Thunder is found in the *Brihadaranyaka—Upanishad*, 5, 1. A translation is found in Deussen's *Sechzig Upanishads des Veda*, p. 489.

408. Cf. Webster, *The White Devil*, V, vi:

> '. . . they'll remarry
> Ere the worm pierce your winding-sheet, ere the spider
> Make a thin curtain for your epitaphs.'

412. Cf. *Inferno*, XXXIII, 46:

> 'ed io senti chiavar l'uscio di sotto
> all' orribile torre.'

Also F. H. Bradley, *Appearance and Reality*, p. 346. 'My external sensations are no less private to myself than are my thoughts or my feelings. In either case my experience falls within my own circle, a circle closed on the outside; and, with all its elements alike, every sphere is opaque to the others which surround it . . . In brief, regarded as an existence which appears in a soul, the whole world for each is peculiar and private to that soul.'

425. V. Weston: *From Ritual to Romance*; chapter on the Fisher King.

428. V. *Purgatorio*, XXVI, 148:

    ' "Ara vos prec per aquella valor

    "que vos condus al som de l'escalina,

    "sovenha vos a temps de ma dolor."

    Poi s'ascose nel foco che li affina.'

429. V. *Pervigilium Veneris*. Cf. Philomela in Parts II and III.

430. V. Gerard de Nerval, Sonnet *El Desdichado*.

432. V. Kyd's *Spanish Tragedy*.

434. Shantih. Repeated as here, a formal ending to an Upanishad. 'The Peace which passeth understanding' is our equivalent to this word.

AFTERWORD

"How It Strikes a Contemporary": no later compre-
hension of a work of art must ever be allowed to
displace the reception it received back then, then and
there, or can it ever exhaust all that we might learn
from how the art first struck: impinged like a blow,
stamped as a coin.

So the indispensable afterword to *The Waste Land*
is that of the reviewers in 1922. If ever a poem was
blessed in its reviewers (even in those who cursed it
roundly or squarely or tangentially), it was *The Waste
Land*. We have become too aware of the fact that great
works of art are often met with philistine outrage, and
this half-truth is often twisted into a gullible supposi-
tion: that outrage must mean that what we have here
is a great work of art. Either way, we have accrued a
healthy distrust of reviewers. Yet meanwhile, insuffi-
ciently acknowledged, there is the other half-truth:
that much of the greatest criticism appears when a
work first appears, with a critical immediacy that gets

hold of the right things even if by the wrong end. There is not a single crucial issue about a poem which does not somewhere strike a nerve, or secure a mention, in the direct response of its first readers. The most important of those first readers are the reviewers, and not only because it is their words which will determine whether the poet's words ever find many readers at all.

By 1922, the thirty-four-year-old T. S. Eliot was already unignorable: the poet of *Prufrock and Other Observations* (1917) and *Poems* (1920) had given delight and consternation—and sometimes delight at the consternation. The author of the new deep diverse astonishment *The Waste Land* (no one before had ever written a poem like it, not even the author of *The Dunciad*, and Eliot himself was not a poet to repeat an accomplishment) was never to become a known quantity, but he was already a known quality. It was those of Eliot's age in America who rose at once to his challenge, challenging his poem as well as thrilling to it.

First came Edmund Wilson, then twenty-seven, already entirely his own man. In *The Dial* (December 1922), Wilson heard—and helped others to hear—

that the poem "sounds for the first time in all their intensity, untempered by irony or disguise, the hunger for beauty and the anguish at living which lie at the bottom of all his work." Wilson, with adept generosity, displayed the anthropological tale and the urban intersection, alive to a consciousness within the poem that "exists not only upon these two planes, but as if throughout the whole of human history." For Wilson, all the objections to the poem that had promptly been clamorously voiced were at once germane and subordinate: they should not be overruled but they had best be overridden. Oh, that *The Waste Land* is bookridden; that it is not a puzzle but a poem; that the feelings are limited or adolescent. True, Wilson concedes, there is something in these complaints, but elsewhere there is more, and always there must be a *But* to come:

> There is a certain grudging margin, to be sure, about all that Mr Eliot writes—as if he were compensating himself for his limitations by a peevish assumption of superiority. But it is the very acuteness of his suffering from this starvation which gives such poignancy to his art.

This, from a gallant review of a supremely taxing and unassimilable poem, had better not be simply accepted as a critical finality, but it has to be gratefully accepted as seizing upon a critical nub. Ungrudging, unpeevish, and very acute, Wilson noticed relations between the things he noticed.

And so, next month, did Elinor Wylie, in the *New York Evening Post* (20 January 1923):

> This power of suggesting intolerable tragedy at the heart of the trivial or the sordid is used with a skill little less than miraculous in *The Waste Land*, and the power is the more moving because of the attendant conviction, that this terrible resembling contrast between nobility and baseness is an agony in the mind of Mr. Eliot of which only a portion is transferred to that of the reader.

Wylie (who was three years older than Eliot) has a settled wisdom that can see the simultaneity of delight and dismay not only in the poem itself but in any true appreciation of it:

In his tortured pity for ugly and ignoble things he sometimes comes near to losing his hardness of outline along with his hardness of heart; his is not a kindly tolerance for weakness and misery, but an obsessed and agonized sense of kinship with it which occasionally leads him into excesses of speech, ejaculations whose flippancy is the expression of profound despair.

It was Conrad Aiken—one year Eliot's junior—who in the *New Republic* (7 February 1923) showed his special gifts as a reviewer-critic by bringing to light the profound imaginative methods of the poem, methods for which necessarily there is a price to be paid. No great poem is ever cheap at the price.

A better critical tour of *The Waste Land* has never been given than Aiken's. He commends the poem, with something of that dry equivocation which his friend Eliot relished:

But also, with this capacity or necessity for being aware in his own way, Mr. Eliot has a haunting, a tyrannous awareness that there have been many other awarenesses before; and that the extent of his own awareness, and perhaps even the nature of it, is a consequence of these.

Aiken may mistake the poem's sympathies, but how economically he identifies what is at stake. "A kind of idolatry of literature with which it is a little difficult to sympathize"? Not necessarily, but this is a crux.

> I think we must, with reservations, and with no invidiousness, conclude that the poem is not, in any formal sense, coherent. We cannot feel that all the symbolisms belong quite inevitably where they have been put; that the order of the parts is an inevitable order; that there is anything more than a rudimentary progress from one theme to another; nor that the relation between the more symbolic parts and the less is always as definite as it should be.

Aiken is very Aristotelian about unity and order— and more than Aristotelian in evoking (twice) the *inevitable*. Yes, all this would need to be argued out, but none of Aiken's caveats could be argued away. The life of the poem is the life of just such enduring contentions, at once creative and critical.

The most pugnacious of those reviewers struck by Eliot was his exact contemporary, that obdurate gentle man and true poet, John Crowe Ransom (*New York Evening Post*, 14 July 1923). Ransom, who feared nothing except that he might lapse into discourtesy, entered upon the poem with mild-mannered courage:

> But what a congenial exercise is furnished the critic by that strange poem, *The Waste Land*. In the first place, everybody agrees beforehand that its author is possessed of uncommon literary powers, and it is certain that, whatever credit the critic may try to take from him, a flattering residue will remain.

But try Ransom does, perfectly creditably, insisting that "Mr. Eliot's performance is the apotheosis of modernity, and seems to bring to a head all the specifically modern errors." This does not have to be modernity run mad, for modernity is already mad. *The Waste Land* is marked by "its extreme disconnection." "To me there are something like fifty parts which offer no bridges the one to the other and which are quite distinct in time, place, action, persons, tone, and nearly all the unities to which art is accustomed." Who would flatly deny what Ransom says? Yet for that to which art is *accustomed* may be something less than that to which art may duly and fiercely accustom us.

Ransom casts his objections in terms which permit us to see his very point under another, more favorable, aspect. "He assails the philosophical or cosmical principles under which we form the usual images of reality." Yes, positively. "We cannot pass, in *The Waste Land*, without a convulsion of the mind from 'O O O O that Shakespeherian Rag,' to 'Shantih shantih shantih.'" But what is the mind, that it should hope never to suffer convulsion or never to learn from convulsion? Yet to put it like this is already to express gratitude not only to Eliot but to Ransom, shaping his judgments finely:

> But it may be put to the credit of Mr. Eliot that he is a man of better parts generally than most of the new poets, as in the fact that he certainly bears no animus against the old poetry except as it is taken for a model by the new poets; he is sufficiently sensitive to its beauties at least to have held on with his memory to some of its ripest texts and to have

introduced them rather wistfully into the forbidding context of his own poems, where they are thoroughly ill at ease.

Pure Eliot, that "ill at ease."

The velvet glove had been thrown down by Ransom's iron hand. It was picked up by Allen Tate, then twenty-three. Tate's reply (*New York Evening Post,* August 4, 1923) said all the right things: that Ransom failed to understand Eliot's purpose in allusion; that regularity of meter is something quite other than unity of form; that Eliot's "ironic attitude" both evinces respect and deserves it. True, true. Yet a bit bland all these years later, with Tate's having come to seem— just because of how much we have learned from such criticism as his—the more conventional of the combatants, Ransom for his part possessing that high critical gift, the power to *ruffle.*

Ruffled feathers were fashionable in England. Never has the (intermittent) superiority of the American critical scene to that of England been more manifest than in the reception of *The Waste Land.* It is true that *The Times Literary Supplement* (October 26, 1922), to which Eliot was a valued contributor, praised the poem not only highly but perceptively ("Life is neither hellish nor heavenly; it has a purgatorial quality. And since it is purgatory, deliverance is possible"). Notice of the *Criterion* printing of the poem was succeeded by a full and appreciative review by Edgell Rickword on September 20, 1923.

But mostly the English reviews have all the peevish superiority of which Eliot himself has been lavishly accused. There was the drawling dawdling of Clive Bell in the *Nation and Athenaeum* (September 22, 1923), prissily precise. At the opposite extreme, there was bluff J. C. Squire in the *London Mercury* (October 1923), bouncing up from table with his mouth full of bread and cheese and saying that he meant to stand no blasted nonsense. Right at the center (King's College, Cambridge, after all), there was F. L. Lucas, an unlovely belletrist who set himself up as the scourge of godforsaken modernism (*New Statesman*, November 3, 1923).

Yet even the pop-eyed reviews have things to teach or to show. There is scarcely an adverse response to *The Waste Land* which the poem has not tauntingly, deliciously, or awe-inspiringly anticipated. Let me close by recalling the most dispiriting and misleading response which the poem ever elicited. It is from someone who could not have been closer to Eliot. I can understand why the man said it; I can understand what personal, social, and creative necessities prompted it; I can respect not just the humorous hope but the grim need to elude pursuit; yet I wish that T. S. Eliot had never committed himself, even in passing, to not being committed to his great poem:

> Various critics have done me the honour to interpret the poem in terms of criticism of the contemporary world, have considered it, indeed, as an important bit of social criticism. To me it was only the relief of a personal and wholly insignificant grouse against life; it is just a piece of rhythmical grumbling.

"To me . . ." But not to me. How about you?

Christopher Ricks
Boston, 1997

Books by T. S. Eliot
available in Harvest paperback editions
from Harcourt Brace & Company

Christianity and Culture
The Cocktail Party
The Confidential Clerk
The Family Reunion
Four Quartets
The Letters of T. S. Eliot, Vol. 1, 1898–1922
Murder in the Cathedral
Old Possum's Book of Practical Cats
Old Possum's Book of Practical Cats, Illustrated Edition
Selected Poems
Selected Prose of T. S. Eliot
The Varieties of Metaphysical Poetry
The Waste Land and Other Poems
The Waste Land, Facsimile Edition

Also available in
Harvest paperback editions

Cats: The Book of the Musical
A Guide to the Selected Poems of T. S. Eliot
by B. C. Southam